The Revolutionary Art of the Future

Rediscovered Poems

HUGH MACDIARMID (Christopher Murray Grieve, 1892–1978) was one of the major poets of the twentieth century and the driving force in modern Scottish literature.

JOHN MANSON is a retired schoolteacher, a poet and a translator. He edited MacDiarmid's *Selected Poems* with David Craig (Penguin, 1970).

DORIAN GRIEVE is Hugh MacDiarmid's grandson, and the co-editor of MacDiarmid's *New Selected Letters* (Carcanet, 2001).

ALAN RIACH is a poet, teacher and critic, Professor and Head of the Department of Scottish Literature at Glasgow University and the general editor of Carcanet's *Collected Works of Hugh MacDiarmid*.

Hugh MacDiarmid, 1949. Photograph by Lida Moser

HUGH MACDIARMID

The Revolutionary Art of the Future

Rediscovered Poems

edited by

John Manson, Dorian Grieve and Alan Riach

CARCANET

in association with

the Scottish Poetry Library

First published in Great Britain in 2003 by
Carcanet Press Limited
Alliance House
Cross Street
Manchester M2 7AQ

in association with the Scottish Poetry Library
5 Crichton's Close
Canongate
Edinburgh EH8 8DT

A CIP catalogue record for this book is available from the British Library
ISBN 1 85754 733 0

The publisher acknowledges financial assistance from
Arts Council England

Typeset in Monotype Bembo by XL Publishing Services, Tiverton
Printed and bound in England by SRP Ltd, Exeter

Contents

Introduction

The Revolutionary Art of the Future is a selection from around 300 poems by Hugh MacDiarmid drawn from the archives of the National Library of Scotland, most of them never published before. MacDiarmid seems not to have submitted them for publication. The title derives from a thirteen-page poem entitled 'Design for the Ballet' in which MacDiarmid develops an argument for revolutionary potential in the art of dance. This poem has not been included. It flounders in digressions and fails; our attempts to select appropriate extracts to give the argument in abbreviated form led to an accumulation of fragments which similarly failed to cohere. But the idea that revolutionary potential may be present in work quietly stored in library archives until it is brought to light is precisely applicable to these poems. Already, this is a controversial little book.

Gerry Cambridge, the editor of the literary periodical *The Dark Horse*, states that it is the best of MacDiarmid's poetry which is important, 'not his impotent political opinions' in his 'self-elected role as pulpiteer and political prophet' (*The Dark Horse*, no.15, Summer 2003, p. 3). Cambridge registers impatience with those 'who not only manage to take such attention-seeking opinions of MacDiarmid seriously, but indeed give them breathing space'. Nevertheless, 'what Douglas Dunn has called this poet's "talent for posthumous controversy" not only lives on, but flourishes'. The 'NB' column in the *Times Literary Supplement* of 18 July 2003 reacted quickly, remonstratively suggesting that people *should* care that MacDiarmid's political opinions were excessively wayward.

At the heart of this, there is an ancient controversy about aesthetics and politics. Volumes of commentary by or about Bertolt Brecht, Walter Benjamin, James Joyce, Ezra Pound – indeed, almost every major writer of the modern movement – have some bearing on it. Benjamin describes the extreme alternatives in his essay, 'The Work of Art in the Age of Mechanical Reproduction' (*Illuminations*, ed. Hannah Arendt, London: Fontana, 1973, p. 244): the far right seek to aestheticise politics (which is why the Nazis had the smartest uniforms) while the far left politicise art. MacDiarmid stands on the left, of course.

Some of his poems express political opinions directly and their literary form bears close analysis as aesthetically progressive. They helped break the tyranny of the pentameter, to paraphrase Ezra Pound. But many are also based on the structures of the Scottish ballads, and in that respect exploit an ancient national tradition in a distinctly modern idiom.

The contradictions of his position are surely no longer surprising. Nor are they unique. For example, Charles Olson once commented of Ezra Pound, 'In language and form he is as forward, as much the revolutionist as Lenin. But in social, economic and political action he is as retrogressive as the Czar' (*Charles Olson & Ezra Pound: An Encounter at St Elizabeths*, ed. Catherine Seelye, New York: Grossman Publishers / Viking, 1975, p. 531). Unless such *contradictoriness* is understood and such complex understanding allowed to inform a sympathetic reading, we will always undervalue Pound, like the critic who simply refused to read him, only referring to him as 'That Fascist from Idaho'. The same is true of MacDiarmid.

The controversy in the British media about these rediscovered poems centred on one entitled 'On the Imminent Destruction of London, June 1940' which prompted a front-page headline in the Glasgow newspaper *The Herald* of 11 April 2003: 'Why MacDiarmid welcomed the London Blitz'. If the date in the title of the poem is to be credited, it was written before the Blitz took place. As an extreme left Republican Nationalist, MacDiarmid's main aim at that time was Scottish independence from the British Empire and not the defence of the Empire. But for four years from early 1942 into 1946 he accepted industrial conscription on Clydeside. The speculation that such a poem would have been treasonable seems unfounded: MacDiarmid was confiding to his notebook. For the poem to be seditious, there would have to have been thought-police. Frighteningly, in the twenty-first century, perhaps that is a more easily imaginable proposition.

The Poetry Editor of *The Herald*, Lesley Duncan, gave a carefully judged and even-handed assessment of the rediscovered poems both on the front page and in a generous full-page article (p. 18) on 11 April. The story was taken up in various quarters of the media and *The Sunday Times* of 13 April (p. 24) quoted comments from the novelist Dame Muriel Spark, who described some of the poems as 'twisted and degrading'. 'Had they been published, he would have been jailed under treachery laws, she said.' In fact, MacDiarmid answers the charge of treachery in NLS MS27033, where he admits that, in general terms, while Scottish patriotism is 'the lost cause of history', his struggle for that cause will continue: '…my country can only gain from my treason / Whatever comes that must be so'.

A further article in *The Sunday Times* of 20 April provided the historian Angus Calder's assessment of MacDiarmid's position, questioning whether he was so detached or eccentric as some had suggested. There is ample literary precedent for denouncing London as the centre of an evil empire: Calder named Blake, Cobbett, Housman, Kipling and Eliot, to whom we might add Dickens and Conrad. Calder recognised that, 'As with all good writers, MacDiarmid's responses to events were multi-layered.'

The impact of the revolutionary and social changes that were taking place when Christopher Grieve was a young man must have been enormous: the First World War, 1914–18, the Irish Easter Rising of 1916, the Russian Revolution of 1917. No other period since that of the French and American Revolutions, at the end of the eighteenth century, represents such a major turning-point in the Western imagination of what society might be in its entirety. Grieve was a journalist in Wales working for Keir Hardie in 1911, covering coalminers' strikes and violent class-warfare. He was a member of Hardie's Independent Labour Party and thus actively involved in the development of the labour movement, creating the foundations of the Labour Party which grew into existence between 1895 and 1906. He was a founder-member of the National Party of Scotland in 1928. In the second two decades of the twentieth century, MacDiarmid's radical politics were very much of their time and the social changes envisioned by them, if radical, must have seemed excitingly practicable. After the Second World War, however, the effectiveness of such radicalism was, perhaps, less easily imaginable.

One of the strongest currents in the book is its anti-war feeling, in poems where the brute facts of soldiering are exposed in horrified sympathy. The sense of human potential wasted so badly is paramount. This was the main theme of *A Drunk Man Looks at the Thistle* (1926) but now it is as if MacDiarmid almost despairs at seeing so much human potential wasted *once again* in the Second World War. In the incendiary London poem, MacDiarmid registers his growing apathy to the shock of modern realities. The poems of this period display an extraordinary capacity for X-raying the most conventional attitudes and taking an opposing view to its most extreme point to see if there's a logical position to be found. MacDiarmid's co-ordinates might seem historical now, but his opinions are not irrelevant to the problems we face today.

Near the end of Iain Banks's novel *Dead Air* (London: Little, Brown, 2002), a statistic is given that commands us to pause and consider: every twenty-four hours about thirty-four thousand children die from malnutrition and disease, in a world that could feed and clothe and treat them all 'with a workably different allocation of resources'. Thinking of the spectacle of the Twin Towers of the World Trade Centre falling on 11 September 2001, Banks's main character comments: 'it's like that image, that ghastly, grey-billowing, double-barrelled fall, repeated twelve times every single fucking day... Full of children.' The narrator says this: 'We feel for the people in the towers... But for the thirty-four thousand, each day? Given our behaviour... you could be forgiven for thinking that most of us just don't give a damn.'

Of course, this is a fictional character speaking in a novel. Critics have a tendency to assume that MacDiarmid's expressed opinions are the utterances of an actual person and it is sometimes difficult to say where, or whether, Hugh MacDiarmid is completely distinct from Christopher Grieve. But it is essential to remember that MacDiarmid is also a name for a fiction, a poetic persona, and that in any case, statements are different when they are made in poems. Things change when you read them in verse. The dissenting voice in MacDiarmid's poems insists that consideration be given to alternative ways of understanding the world, ways of seeing that are different from those endorsed by popular media and social conformity.

In the essay 'Scotland: Full Circle', published in *Whither Scotland? A Prejudiced Look at the Future of a Nation* (ed. Duncan Glen, London: Victor Gollancz, 1971, pp. 233–50 (p. 234)), MacDiarmid notes that when people get used to social conventions they resist deep analysis of society's forms: 'The forms of accepted analysis, and the judgements that go with them, are part of the deep accommodation to an orthodox consciousness.' In many of the poems in this book, MacDiarmid emphasises that people should not be seduced into believing only what familiar discourse and capitalist moguls would have us assume.

There was never anything very surreptitious about this. As a poet, journalist and committedly full-time writer, MacDiarmid was continually articulating political positions. This makes George Orwell's noting of MacDiarmid's politics in the blacklist of Reds he supplied to the British Foreign Office in 1949 remarkable in its redundancy. Orwell was advising a cryptic group named the Information Research Department about people he thought should not be trusted to write anti-Communist propaganda during the Cold War. It must have been pellucidly clear that MacDiarmid would not have written anti-Communist propaganda for the British government but Orwell emphasises the point, describing him as a 'Dissident Communist but reliably pro-Russian' (Timothy Garton Ash, 'Love, death and treachery', *The Guardian Review*, 21 June 2003, pp. 4–7.) As far as political subterfuge was concerned, he was a liability. Tom Macdonald (the novelist Fionn Mac Colla), who, in 1930, was involved in the attempt to form a Scottish nationalist activist group which MacDiarmid also supported, summed up MacDiarmid's tendency towards the explicit in his autobiography *Ro Fhada Mar So A Tha Mi / Too Long in This Condition* (Thurso: Caithness Books, 1975, p. 94): he was never good about keeping secrets. 'As for C.M. Grieve's part in the matter,' Mac Colla wrote, 'one can only say that conspiracy was not his métier. Neither by temperament nor habit of life was he suited to it.'

★ ★ ★

The poems were collected by John Manson, an independent scholar, a retired schoolteacher, a poet and translator and the co-editor with David Craig of the 1970 edition of MacDiarmid's *Selected Poems*.

He had long been aware that there were unpublished or forgotten MacDiarmid poems. In fact, MacDiarmid had once asked him if one of his poems had been published. But the number of poems awaiting rediscovery came as a revelation. Some of them had in fact come to light through the research of scholars such as Kenneth Buthlay, Patrick Crotty, Dorian Grieve and Alan Riach, but beginning in 2001, Manson began to make a thorough search of the collection in the National Library of Scotland as part of a wider enquiry into the literature and politics of the left in Scotland in the 1930s and MacDiarmid's life and work at that time.

The manuscript poems – in typescript, pen, pencil, biro – were on single or double sheets in folders sorted by the library, or in bound notebooks. Some were fair copies; others had scorings-out, substitutions and words difficult to read. In all, over twenty folders and notebooks are represented in the collection. MS27031 provided more than any other source.

There are a number of possible reasons why the poems remained unpublished: MacDiarmid may have forgotten he had written them (as he says of the poems collected in *A Lap of Honour*); opportunities for publication might not have existed at the time of writing; his papers may have been unavailable to him when they were in storage after his leaving the Shetland Islands; some may have been noted down, to be revised at a later date; some may have been discarded as unfinishable or abandoned as unsuccessful. Also, some poems may have been considered seditious during the Second World War and it is difficult to think where he might have submitted them for publication. It may have been a consideration that to have published them in a little magazine of the time might have led to that magazine's closure.

Some of the poems show a range of responses to the build-up to the Second World War – satires on Goering and Hitler, an attack on the Munich agreement, protests against conscription and the treatment of 'heroes' of the First World War. After the war started MacDiarmid showed sympathy with the French people at the fall of France, and he espoused Scottish independence as a blow against the British Empire. He had nothing to say in defence of that Empire. In the National Library MS27142 f.27v, this fragment speaks eloquently of his essential position:

The picture of Casement hanged, and Connolly taken out on a stretcher and executed, are two of the great rallying points of my spirit in its eternal and immeasurable hatred of everything English.

An unexpected find too long to be included is a poem describing Hitler (MS27105 ff.8–15), a man 'inhibited by a kind of fear / Of understanding and mental exposition', who felt no kinship with 'any / Great intellectual figure of the past' and who 'would chop up a Stradivarius violin / To grill a steak':

The perfect representative of a political movement
Which has no real belief
Except in the act of ruling.
And no principle except
To have an answer for every situation…

MacDiarmid scorns this position:

Humanity's despair in the face of its problems
Has created this type
And sane reflection will remove it again.
Seldom has there been a purer example of the politician
– That is, a man who uses everything,
Objects, ideas, people,
As a means to an end.
This is his mysterious and repellant strength
– His deep and essential lack of love and affection,
Finding its disguise, but not its compensation,
In a thick layer of sentimentality and self-pity
And in a longing for his fellow men
That cannot be satisfied
Because he is incapable of giving.
He has nothing to give.

This principle of giving evidently animated MacDiarmid and infuriated him again and again when he encountered its lack. In a poem that seems to have been addressed to one of his son Michael's schoolteachers in the Shetlands, he reprimands the stultifying rigour of the school system (NLS MS27105 ff.23–5). He wishes for a postgraduate course, not in 'book knowledge' but 'in the handling of plastic minds' – to keep them 'susceptible and flexible' rather than 'rigid and arrogant':

What are the glories
Of the free spirit that seeks
To a creature like you,
Gaoler rather than teacher
Like almost all of your kind?

Then he extrapolates this to a general observation:

The whole of life is how to make people aware.
We are all blind, deaf, and dumb
To too many things both inside us and outside us.
All that teachers like you do to children
Is to 'settle them into life' – make them feel
That disillusion, boredom, restless activity
And all the rest of it, are part of life
And have to be accepted. Why struggle?

But perhaps the most surprising discoveries are those poems in which the Gospels and the Psalms are quoted and acknowledged, where MacDiarmid aligns himself with a spiritual vision and a quasi-religious simplicity of utterance. If the polemical poems risk wearying readers, these risk an unsteady balance between Blakean freshness and occasional banalities no sense of authenticity can relieve:

> What we look for
> Is the beauty that is manifest:
> The sea all ablaze with gold and sapphire
> And glittering spray,
> The snow lit by the rosy dawn
> Or sunset hues,
> The silver of the stream,
> The world of wonder in a flower.

In this long untitled fragment (MS27033 ff.1–5), MacDiarmid moves from quotations from the Gospels of John, Matthew, the Psalms, Ephesians, Isaiah, to praise of Lenin and the Soviet poet Mayakovsky and Scottish patriotism, ending on the declaration that the struggle towards Scottish national self-expression is a struggle against the greed of the system of world-exploitation enacted by the British Empire. If there is a war to defend small nations, 'in defence of liberty and culture' then it must begin 'At home'.

Other poems show that MacDiarmid went on responding to public events such as the execution of the Rosenbergs in 1953 or the war in Viet-Nam contrasted with the disaster at Aberfan in 1966, when a mountainside of coal-slag avalanched down on a school, killing 144 people, 116 of them children. These poems are a kind of journalism-in-verse. 'Of the Cheka's Horrors' appears to be his reply to criticism of three lines in the 'First Hymn to Lenin'. These lines, referring to the Cheka, the Extraordinary Commission for Repression Against Counter-Revolution, Speculation and Desertion, are often quoted by lazy critics as if they provided incontrovertible proof that MacDiarmid was insanely murderous, utterly callous and politically inept:

> What maitters 't wha we kill
> To lessen that foulest murder that deprives
> Maist men o' real lives?

In the context of the poem, the emphasis falls on the desire to help most men get real lives, just as it does at the end of 'On a Raised Beach' where the aspiration to get a life worth having is made despite the geological scale of the opposition. There is no denying the violence of MacDiarmid's expression, however, but it should always be remembered that these lines are directly contradicted by 'Ballad of Aun, King of Sweden', written in June 1940 (*Complete Poems*, vol. 1, pp. 720–21). In this poem MacDiarmid compares Aun's slaughter of his nine sons to governments' slaughter of their people and concludes:

> But when will the people rise and slay
> The ubiquitous Aun of State Murder to-day?
> Realising murder is foulest murder no matter
> What individual or body for what end does the slaughter!

(Acknowledgements are due to the critic Hugh Mackay for pointing this out to John Manson.) In another poem, 'The Poet as Prophet', written in the late 1930s (*Complete Poems*, vol. 2, pp. 1372–6), MacDiarmid shows he was well aware of '… that cardinal sin / Of mistaking means for ends'.

Throughout his life, MacDiarmid impetuously took up positions which later became difficult to justify. For example, his articles 'Plea for a Scottish Fascism' and 'Programme for a Scottish Fascism' were written immediately after he had read Pietro Gorgolini's *The Fascist Movement in Italian Life* (London, 1923) and he quoted from it with and without acknowledgement. (Thanks are due to Dr Bob Purdie for this reference.) This contradictoriness might be considered hypocrisy in a politician, irresponsible in a teacher, unjustifiable in journalism, but it is a practice MacDiarmid exercised to his advantage self-consciously as a poet. He says as much in the poem entitled 'The Logic of Contradiction' which relates the practice back to Keats's 'negative capability', and in a letter to the Scottish nationalist sculptor and poet Pittendrigh MacGillivray, dated 1 November 1926, he spells it out: 'In scores of directions I find two very different impulses animating me – 1/ to avoid coming to any conclusions on certain fundamental matters: i.e. moral and ethical problems; and 2/ to experiment with the artistic expression of every different attitude I can conceive, i.e. to make every different attitude as wholly mine at a given time as I possibly can and find to what extent I can make a "convincing" poem of it' (Hugh MacDiarmid, *The Letters*, ed. Alan Bold, London: Hamish Hamilton, 1984, p. 331).

He was not the only poet to do this. The American poet Robert Creeley once remarked that the influential essay 'Projective Verse' written by his friend Charles Olson may have had a terrific influence but it was not intended as a 'prescriptive poetics': 'I remember Irving Layton, actually, when he and Charles finally met, he apparently said to Charles, "Well, I didn't think what you were doing had much to do with projective verse." And Charles said, "I wrote that one day, Irving, and the next day I wrote something else!"' (Alan Riach, 'An Interview with Robert Creeley', *Australasian Journal of American Studies*, vol. 15, no. 1, July 1996, pp. 31–43 (p. 39)). This recollects the famous quotation in which Walt Whitman praises his own capacity for self-contradiction, with which MacDiarmid felt considerable affinity.

Self-contradictoriness might lead to a kind of disengagement, however, a distancing from direct concern. In another poem from the Second World War, MacDiarmid is explicit about the need to refuse to be 'desensitized'. 'Hardihood, valour, thorough and most versatile knowledge, / And sheer determination' he says, are the things he has learned to prize most from past experience. However, only sheer determination will be of help in the current situation, provided we don't 'steel ourselves' – which would 'serve for mere survival only':

Any man worth the name would rather die
And be done with it. We must not be desensitized
– Must not desensitize ourselves – whatever befalls,
But learn while seeing and feeling no less
(Without knowing it perhaps at the time
Or letting it affect us no more
Than if we were blind and insentient)
Simply not to react at all.

That is the only way.

(MS 27095 7v, 8; published in the *Scottish Literary Journal*, vol. 27, no. 1, 2000)

★ ★ ★

The poems gathered here take us through most of MacDiarmid's career, from the 1920s to the 1970s, but they date predominantly from the 1930s and 1940s. They are arranged in a loosely chronological sequence, with dates where available noted in the Acknowledgements at the end of the book.

The poem which gave us our title seems characteristically wild, yet it is worth sketching out MacDiarmid's wayward proposition, for there is a sound intention behind it. He begins by noting that people will sacrifice a lot for the pleasure of taking part in 'intense common activity' such as the disagreeable behaviour of modern crowds. We need not face this fact only with a stoical regard for its truth but should do so also with the hope that 'if we understand / Instead of denounce our fellows / We may discover / How to make this fact / Serve the construction / Of a better state of things'.

> The task and problem of the intelligent is then
> Not to denounce mob-emotion
> But to construct social patterns
> In which that emotion may express itself...

Thus, 'The wise man dances / What the bad man does.' And:

> The wise society brings itself together
> With a beautiful pattern
> While the base society can only do so
> In mob violence or war frenzy.

Given this premise, MacDiarmid points out that music hall entertainment is a vitally sensitive location in which to study people selecting what their emotions require – far more so than cinema, which gives what 'film kings' dictate. But even more than music hall, the most sensitive, flexible and immediate recorder of human need is dance, and especially ballet. It may be that this developing form is the first 'Tentative experimental unconscious effort / Of democracy to save itself'. Modern dance, he argues, must be essentially an art of the people, a vernacular movement, free in imaginative range and distinct from 'arbitrary formalism' – an expression of 'true romanticism':

> The sole function of form
> In a simple and natural art of this sort
> Is to ensure

That the material makes sense.
Obviously this is more difficult
Than to build a synthetic makeshift
To titillate the aesthete
For it demands roots in life.
Ready-made formulas will not serve
Any more than second-hand material will.
Form is not merely arrangement,
It is action;
Not the juggling of passive ingredients
But the projection of living material.

Describing the dance art of Anna Sokolow, MacDiarmid asserts that it 'should grow out of the lives of the masses / And have value for them' rather than the 'refinements of taste / Of a limited audience of connoisseurs'. The poem ends with two skaters on the ice, describing great arcs without looking at each other, meeting at an exact point in the musical phrase and continuing the dance together: 'the dramatisation / Of motion itself' (NLS MS27031 ff.79–91).

This vision of dance as a model for social organisation agrees with the hopefulness of MacDiarmid's life's effort. In another surprising discovery, MacDiarmid affirms 'the ethic of Jesus, / Based really upon the eternity of Love'. To the extent that Christ's ethic was conceived as 'an interim code for the guidance of the elect / During the short time before the end of the world' MacDiarmid opposes it as something 'based on world-negation / Whereas we must base ours on world-affirmation'. Nevertheless, Christ's ethic of love itself, MacDiarmid concludes, remains 'independent of the world-view / In which it was framed' and 'Authoritative for us all' (MS27033 f.14).

The Irish writer Nuala O'Faolain once attended a performance of

Beethoven's only opera, *Fidelio*, in the company of the great Communist teacher Arnold Kettle. When the curtain came down O'Faolain was crying. 'Why is ensemble singing so beautiful?' she asked. And Kettle replied: 'People would be like that all the time, if they could.'

Whether you believe in the Socialism behind that sentiment or not, the vision it implies is one of hope – 'Society perfected, free of deformations and oppressions. People so freed would communicate perfectly, as they do when they sing together in opera. Music prefigures whatever there can be of human and social perfection. There is an ideal, perfect, shape, behind the appearance of things. There is the possibility of perfect communication, and to try to establish social justice is a way of moving towards it' (*Are You Somebody? The Life and Times of Nuala O'Faolain*, London: Sceptre, 1996, pp. 131–2).

★ ★ ★

This book will not make friends of his enemies and we never hoped that it would, but we might wish for a more considered reading than the reflex reactions some of the more provocative pieces seem to invite:

> The idea of a female sex
> Is a little puzzling, no doubt,
> But if this is how human beings want
> To perpetuate their species, well it's their look-out!
>   (NLS Acc.11451 n.d.; published in *The Scottish Literary Journal*,
>   vol. 27, no. 1, 2000)

The sense of humour in this may seem offensive – or else merely quaint – but it's certainly uncommon. A fragment in another poem likens Scotland ever since Flodden to a woman with nothing to do 'but watch / Her mind narrow as her hips broaden' (NLS MS27032 f.199). Yet the sympathy in 'Mary Reflects' and the self-scrutiny exposed in 'A Married Man' open depths of insight and understanding about human sexuality and desire: a broader sympathy is needed.

In the third of the anthologies of Scottish poets he edited in the 1920s, *Northern Numbers*, MacDiarmid quite clearly foregrounds his proto-feminist commitment: of the twenty contributors, ten are men and ten are women. No poet has been more politically correct before the term had been invented. And sometimes MacDiarmid has the unforgivable knack of being very funny. When they work, the jokes startle:

> To drink is a Christian diversion
> Unknown to the Turk or the Persian
> I don't like X's that's true
> Yet give credit where credit is due.
>> (NLS Acc. 11451 n.d.; published in *The Scottish Literary Journal*,
>> vol. 27, no. 1, 2000)

The range of subjects in this little book is extraordinary: there are thoughtful, provocative poems about sexuality and identity, marriage and divorce. For example, 'A Married Man' gives his quiet response to his divorce and the separation from his children in contrast to the vituperative letters he addressed to his first wife which are published in the *New Selected Letters* (Manchester: Carcanet, 2001). As well as these, there are poems to do with personal occasions and moments of private reflection, noticing weeds growing in the grass near a grave, having a curious meal in Edinburgh, getting water from the well.

Some of these poems extend MacDiarmid's anatomical self-scrutiny to new areas of tenderness, exhilarating affirmation and questioning. There are comic squibs, short, quick, immediately accessible, rhyming satires, on the uselessness of men, the hypocrisy of the Church, the complacency of the bourgeoisie. This is the MacDiarmid who once said there were only two problems in the world – ignorance and stupidity. Ignorance you can do something about, but stupidity…

In these poems, MacDiarmid uses healthily derisive laughter to deal with stupidity and challenges the ignorant to learn more.

At the heart of MacDiarmid's work is what Marshall Walker calls 'the intrinsic optimism of curiosity', what Harvey Oxenhorn describes as 'a manger-faith' and, however naive it must appear at times, a sympathetic, bracing and zestful appetite for life:

> How glorious to live! Even in one thought
> The wisdom of past times to fit together
> And from the luminous minds of many men
> Catch a reflected truth: as, in one eye,
> Light, from unnumbered worlds and farthest planets
> Of the star-crowded universe, is gathered
> Into one ray.

(NLS MS27145 f.10r in ink)

This is a truly dissenting voice, still shocking twenty-five years after his death. Lesley Duncan, in her article in *The Herald*, wrote that MacDiarmid was 'staking all his spiritual substance on the art of poetry'. This book shows how high the stakes were.

A Note on the Texts

The editors have taken care to produce a book which should be immediately accessible with a minimum of apparatus. Only a few notes, references and glosses seemed required on the page and almost all the Scots words are easily inferred by English-speaking readers. John Manson transcribed the texts from the typescripts or manuscripts in the National Library; Dorian Grieve scrutinised particular manuscripts to confirm less easily deciphered words; all three editors selected and arranged the texts. Helen Lloyd scanned and checked the poems when they were entered to disk and hard-drive.

Many of the poems seem to have been written quickly and never revised. Some small emendations have been made silently, such as the question mark inserted at the end of the first line of 'Culloden' and the second 'the' in line 9 of '*from* The Monarch of the Glen'. Also in 'Culloden', the word 'held' was chosen when other possibilities included 'press'd' or 'pent' or 'penn'd'. We felt it was unnecessary to clutter the poems with square brackets and editorial details in the present edition.

Not all the poems in the National Library's MacDiarmid collection are by MacDiarmid. Even manuscripts in his hand may have been copied from other writers and some verses may have been attributed to him mistakenly. Regretfully, we have had to drop a hilarious song listing the great 'Chairlies' of history, including Chairlie Marx and Chairlie Magne, prompted by the Prince of Wales going up to Trinity College, Cambridge, in 1967: 'über alles / Our braw wee princie in the palace'. Though the verses are catalogued by the National Library among MacDiarmid's papers, the typeface, paper and a reference in a letter led us to conclude that in fact they weren't written by MacDiarmid but by Andrew Tannahill, who wrote a number of satirical songs in similar vein. MacDiarmid would have approved.

Also regretfully, we chose not to include stand-alone poems which have been already published as part of larger works. For example, an exhilarating sixteen-line poem beginning 'On towards the calculus of ideas...' was found to be part of *In Memoriam James Joyce*, in print in the *Complete*

Poems (vol. 2, pp. 802–3). It is worth noting that MacDiarmid saw such poems as valid individual items yet also, simultaneously, as parts of a longer work-in-progress. Similarly, 'The Whole Keyboard' looks as though it should be part of *The Kind of Poetry I Want*, but we have allowed it to appear here as a separate poem or a distillation of that longer work. Curiously related to this is the poem 'Like a Particle of Bone'. The first four lines of this are identical to those of a 74-line poem of October 1938 entitled 'When the Gangs Came to London' which was sent to the novelist Catherine Carswell and turned up among Carswell's papers. When Margery Palmer McCulloch of Glasgow University's Department of Scottish Literature rediscovered this poem, it was published in the Edinburgh newspaper *The Scotsman* on Thursday 25 November 1999. The 13-line poem published here, however, is much more intense, bitter and hard than the 74-line verse polemic and deserves recognition for its own purposive integrity. We believe that the same might be said for all the poems collected in *The Revolutionary Art of the Future*.

John Manson, Dorian Grieve and Alan Riach

The Secret Voice

My voice is like a bairn
   – O wad that it could tell
The hauf that's in my brain
   And body – to mysel!

For Language is a young thing
   But Flesh is auld – and mind;
And words for what we are,
   Or ken, are ill to find.

And fegs! for Life and Lear
It's hard to thole to hear
The silly havers Thocht
At best can mak' o' ocht.

Yet whiles through words can brak'
   A music that can gliff
   Body and brain as if
Their benmaist secrets spak'.

Mary Reflects

It is difficult to keep from a man the bitter knowledge
That the first great feeling of love has gone,
Leaving in its wake something less than love
Yet not just kindness alone.

There is no exact word for this emotion
Or frame of mind; nevertheless it is what
Most wives have to content themselves with
– The great and beautiful fire subsiding
To a few warm coals, providing
A kind of comfort – but no more than that!

The Lilypond

The lilypond is lush with green leaves
Clustered so thickly
That there is scarcely any water to be seen
And the goldfish of which one catches
Occasional shining glimpses
Spend their lives in a perpetual twilight.

I peer into the green-hidden depths.
The flicker of a golden tail answers me
And a faint sidling movement of the lilypads
Gives token of a darting fish beneath.

Poor devils! Fish like the dusk,
But this is living in Cimmerian darkness.
I wonder if I can pull off a few of the leaves
– But the lily stems are tough as thongs of leather
Or like a plaiting of endless black snakes.

Mother

It was an early bright morning when the harmony of nature
Was resting on the world that I looked and saw
A noble old image appear in my eyes – as if
Scotland was coming towards me, a little gay breeze
From the blue sea moving her lovely gray hair.

The bourgeoisie of Scotland may have lost all sense
Of human feeling; but surely your image
Will live forever as an example
Of the noble tradition of Scottish woman
Or, dying, leave proselytes among your friends
That I know, and, unknowing, that I love.

My Follies Are My Studies

I have great faults and many reprimand me
For this, for that, and for the other
But this life feeds my lamp which as you see
Would die out otherwise. So they need not bother.
My follies are my studies. You cannot draw
The wine off the cask all the time and put nothing in.
This is my way of replenishing my brain
When I have exhausted it.

To Christine

The sea, my dear, is such a little thing.
A day will come when you – you, too! –
Will see the ocean that affrights you now
As 'twere a bead of dew.

The highest hills will be as grains of sand
Beneath your feet one day, my dear,
But I am glad they tower above you now,
And will, for many a year.

If Christ Rose Today

If Christ rose today
Said a Fleet Street man
So complete is our sway
We could dish his plan
Not a word would get out
He might as well have lain still
Our conspiracy of silence would kill
His resurrection at birth – and love no doubt.

It's a Fine Thing

It's a fine thing for bairns aince a year
To gang singing frae door to door
And get a richt welcome frae ilka gudewife
And fruit, cakes, and sweets galore.

Aye, Hogmanay is a splendid thing
No' just for bairns but for grown-ups tae
– Remindin' them that a'thing worth ha'en
Is got free gratis in a similar way.

For life's a Hogmanay no' aince a year
But ilka day – and a' onybody has and is
Is juist the share they've been lucky to get
Frae God's universal *Bescherung* I wis.

Rise up auld wife and shak your feathers
Is the cry o' the bairns on Hogmanay
But it's no' the source o' the gifts that's asleep
The receivin' end ligs unconscious the day.

Bescherung: giving of presents.

Everything in Edinburgh

Everything in Edinburgh
Is smooth as owl's grease –
I used to be a working reporter.
I know things like these.

But why I should be given frozen steak
At a meal designed for duck.
Fancy serving wild rice and sour-sweet red cabbage
With baby beef. Something's come unstuck.

But that's the sort of thing that happens
In Edinburgh. I'm sorry we went.
And the wine was white till I got up
And personally bought three bottles of Moulin au Vent.

Bourgeois Poetry

Pallid from disconnection with any sensible world,
Wilted flowers in a vase no one has supplied with water,
– The flower without the root, ideas without being,
The clipped and savourless speech of a spent kind,
Saying less than they mean, murmuring with small mouths,
Understating most gallantly, most nobly;
With themes calling for trumpets, for woodwinds, for bells;
But what do we hear? – Mere lips, mere teeth, clipping sound!

A Man's a Man

There was a massive St Bernard and a sinewy greyhound
And a wise old collie, when breaking through
Came a hideous dachshund
Proclaiming 'But I'm like a liver sausage gone bad, I'm a dog too!'

There was Mohammed and Plato and Shakespeare and Dante,
And Spinoza and Hegel – 'but I'll tell you flat'
Cried J.G. Smith, wine and spirit merchant, Milngavie
'A man's a man for a' that'.

Holiday Plan

I'm a Scotsman I'll go North – not South.
Since I long for a more rugged sea
For turbulence and grandeur, for blackness too,
An outer severity enclosing a subtlety
Of emotion more seductive because more elusive
Than anything the South can give.
Not Blackpool, not Brighton, not Torquay
But Shetland then, and the Faroes for me.

Yea I'll go to one of the little wild isles.
That always does me good
Since I'm a Scotsman with the sea
And the wind and the rocks in my blood.

On an Opponent of Scots Literature

or, against the contention that black is white and white black

'The Scots tradition in literature
Has been dying for half-a-millennium'
(Not a natural death, but supplanted,
Starved and suppressed by the English!)
'And is now quite moribund.
Let go that "nonsensical trash"
In Sir Walter Scott's phrase', said the nyauf*
In an aesthetic Edinburgh drawing-room
To a crowd that matched the colour-scheme,
'Our past is unmeaning
And therefore quite unrelated
To any prospective literary developments.'
(Besides, efforts along that line divert
Attention from his own august achievements,
And Willa's – don't forget Willa's.
Always the little gentleman!)
'Moreover, to occupy oneself
With a resurrection of the dead past
Is a purely Fascist line
Found in Germany and Italy alone.'
(This Fascistic significance is the reason, of course,
Why, suggesting the inclusion of Afrikaans
In the English curriculum at the Cape,
Sir Thomas Holland is yet bitterly opposed

To a Chair of Scottish Literature
In Edinburgh University
– Strange that anti-Fascism should here alone be at one
With the English Ascendancy policy! –)

★ nyauf – insignificant [person] [MacDiarmid's note]

Willa's: Willa Muir, novelist and wife of Edwin Muir.
Sir Thomas Holland: Vice Chancellor and Principal of Edinburgh University, 1929–44.

My Ambition

Ah, this is my ambition indeed:
To rise up among all the insipid, unsalted, rabbity, endlessly hopping
                                                              people

And sing a great song of our Alba bheadarrach
– An exuberant, fustigating, truculent, polysyllabic
Generous, eccentric, and incomparably learned song
And so bring fresh laurels to deck the brows
Of Alba bheadarrach is Alba-nuadhaichte, ath-leasaichte, is
                                                ath-bheothaichte.

bheadarrach: beloved.
is: and.
ath-nuadhaichte: newborn.
ath-leasaichte: newly improved.
ath-bheothaichte: new come to life.

The Whole Keyboard

The whole keyboard – all the way
From *le mot juste* to the Omnific word.

Feats in multiple definition of a Mencius raised to the Nth
– A super-Joycean *Ulysses*, not of a day in Dublin
But of the whole of time from the first day to the last
Everywhere on the Earth at once.

Candlesmas

O hoo can you keep in the air sae lang
Muckle black craw, fleein' dooble like that?
Craw and shadow, no' to lay haud o',
A lass may doot if you'll ever be caught.

It seems I may trail you owre the grey hills
Yont bogl-day on to the Beltane and yet
Your fiky wings winna scart the grund.
O let doon your feet, you brute, and sit!

For I'm weary weary wi' followin' you
And fain to ken whaur oor hoose'll be
Tho' I'm glad you haud to the island still
And haena thocht to big in the sea.

bogl-day: a feast day on which a 'buggle' or great bannock is baked for each
member of the family.

from *The Dark Whirling Dun*

A name for various dusky-coloured flies used in angling, and for artificial flies imitating these.

By Whuchulls

Even as at the fishin' I find
My best catches are aye won
When the fly I wampish
Is the Dark Whirlin' Dun
That'll serve for Leviathan nae doot
As weel as for ony troot.

★★★

Sae when I scrieve ayont mysel'
Drawin' frae sources no' to tabulate
In this world because they're no' to this world
A' I need is some vague idea, adminiculate,
Since I'm nae amateur,
Wi' a' my knowledge and poo'er
Arrayed like a mare in season;
That – and this wee moth-like lure
That may look ludicrously sma'
Compared wi' the supreme quarry
But has a wonderfu' poo'er o' blackness
                              For a' that.

Creative artists dinna need
A course set clear afore them.
Gie me the men wha feel blin' fog
To stupendous poo'ers restore them.

Wha ride wi' a' forgotten
Except what they lo'e best,
And *that*, shapeless like the wind,
Openin' nae way through the rest.

Something vaguer, deeper, commoner
Than ony form they choose
And exult, tho' ithers canna
Ken hoo deep is their Muse.

★★★

The onrush o' the waters
Affects your thocht
And you're carried faurer
Than you mebbe socht or ocht.

And as wi' the waters
In the river's course
Your mind draws tributaries
Frae ilka possible source

And carries them a'
Doun to a common sea,
Losing little en route
In its jealous fury.

Losing little and aye
Gaining faur mair
Till it yields up at last
A deemless store there.

★★★

The Dark Whirlin' Dun – aye, weel I ken
Sic sudden tornadoes o' the spirit
Wi' their utter disregaird o' tradition,
Comfort, kindliness, material possessions
Personal or communal, and welcome their mission
Which means it's noo the Void itsel' I'm fishin'.
Shair proof o' immortality, sin' nane
But an immortal being could hae
Sic recklessness and lunacy, as kyths in a man
When he draws irrationality frae this fitless sink
That repels a' else, appalled, frae its brink.
It's as gin I turn aff the artificial licht
In the close wee room o' consciousness men spend their days in
And, thinkin' mysel made blin', look up to see
The windas open and a' the constellations blazin'.

wampish: flourish.
adminicular (?): auxiliary.

The Mouse that Bit the Cat

O the gled's whussle o' a man-free thing!
H'ye ne'er seen ocht you hedna seen afore,
Nor seen nor dreamt ocht like it ev'n,
(The commonest thing in life whiles looks like that!)
Serrin' nae purpose, answerin' nae desire,
Flatterin' nae sense, but at cross-purposes
Wi' a' you'd seen, thocht, needit; or desired,
Until it seemed, gin that could really be,
A' else, the nature o' your bein', was vain;
And syne jaloused Man's final poo'ers'll ken
Less than a'e side o' thocht and that at odds
E'en wi' the seen the unseen's to his een –
Aye, watched your memory and imagination
Faith, hope, and a'thing that combine to gi'e
A meanin' to the things o' earth collapse,
And kent that there is nocht that winna brak
Sooner or later frae the darknin' mass
O' a' man's thocht like lichtnin' frae a clood?
Man's destiny when it meets Creation's fegs,
Is unco like the moose that bit the cat.

gled's whussle: the whistle of a kite or hawk; an expression of triumph.

Ex Nihil

It shall be wi' my verses henceforth
  As it is here again wi' the Earth
That has naething but bare rock left
  And yet kens nae dearth.

The variety o' form is nae less,
The sense o' sameness nae mair
– Nay, Earth's endless resource is seen better
  Noo there's naething else there.

In the welter o' secondary shapes
True character was sairly owrelaid.
Here the essential spirit triumphs again
Wi' nae adventurous aid.

A' the sae-ca'd progress o' men,
Industry, science, never did ocht
But hide the real nature o' poetry
That save its ain sel' needs nocht.

Working at Last

He wouldn't do a hand's turn
As long as he lived, she said,
So I had him cremated
      Once he was dead.

He's been of more use since,
For you see, my dear,
These are his ashes
      In the egg-timer here.

The Logic of Contradiction

I am full of Keats's negative capability
(With due and complete awareness of the logical machinery
I am using at any moment – and of the alternatives
I might use, or can at least imagine using)
– The power of holding in my mind all manner of doubts and
                                                    contradictions
With no impatience to find solutions in me,
To find a key, a panacea, an open sesame, a single
Solution to all problems, or to follow
One single philosophic or religious line,
Accepting it as the right and only one for me,
But influenced to some extent by everything with which
I come in contact, something in me remains uninfluenced,
Something capable of holding all these simultaneously
And building them up into a complexity
Making for myself not a simplex
But a complex conception of all things
– Not trying to present myself as a complete, organised whole
With the corners rubbed smooth, the irregularities removed,
The discrepancies, irrelevancies, and peccadillos left unmentioned,
But as a fluid, mercurial, many-sided, many-dimensional personality,
Who yet understands and can convey in words
These many sides and dimensions.

I Thank God Most

I thank God most
For complete strangers, and all
The things I will never see or hear.

Of the Cheka's Horrors

Yes. They are murderers and thieves.
The rulers of men have all been that.
I admit all you say and far more
Of the Cheka's atrocities. – What?
Then I can't as a Bolshevik pass?
That's just why I am, you ass!
Can't one have one's likes and dislikes
In theft and murder as well
As in other things – allow me
My own special variety of Hell.

Even Death Has a Home-life

Even Death has a home-life. It doesn't
Strike suddenly out of nowhere.
Death, where do you live when you're alone?
All over the place. Now here. Now there,
Like a bird that flies from bough to bough.
But where are you now? Oh, where are you now?

Bedrock

There's nae trees here.
If this happened elsewhere
Something needfu' 'ud seem
To be missin' there.

Nae human inhabitants,
Nae rivers, nae trees,
But this island's complete,
And richer withoot these.

Sae let vain appearances
Frae my verses disappear.
O' ony incompleteness
Or want I've nae fear.

I've as little need here
For a' ither folk
As the sea and the wind and the light
And the skerries o' naked rock.

Vementry

Scrotum-tightening flood,
Nae wumman e'er caressed like this,
Naething is closed to you.
You gi'e me matchless bliss
  Gettin' nane frae me,
  Carin' nocht for me,
  Ready at ony meenut
To whelm me senseless in your abyss.

Sae I've seen rise
In madness and disease
Incomparable joys, as frae bare rock,
Shaggy moorland and dark seas
  Colour and licht
  Can suddenly
  As they are da'en noo
Miracle upon miracle gie's.

Or harsh as cast-iron
Or cauld as drivin' snaw
Or fierce wi' white foam, as a bird's feathers
Whiles in a hurricane blaw,
Now you are streaked and veined
Wi' shadows o' the grape
As gin a hand tenderly stroked you
And you felt as I feel ana'.

The shadows on the snaw
Are blue, blue as the lift,
But you are a different blue
And on the horizon drift
Blue as a hedge-sparrow's egg
No' blue but sun-gold
– Sun-gold – and toss
Your bubbles up like a fairy gift.

'Twixt the ridges of rock
In your clear level I lay me
As your ghostly fish dae, nose upstream,
Tail wavin' lazily
And my thochts are the grey forms that shift
Inch by inch to a'e side or the ither
And, disappearin' and back again, forever
In the same transparent lodgin' I see.

Vementry: an island of Sandsting parish, in the Shetland Islands, on the south side of St Magnus Bay, within a furlong of the nearest point of the mainland, and three and a quarter miles east of Papa Stour.

When I Go to the Well

When I go to the well carrying my water pails
The terns with their shrill cries hover over me
Lovely little white and grey birds with long tails
That shut in a point and then flick open in a narrow V
They drop on me suddenly pecking the crown of my hat
Sometimes three or four together – then wheeling off, high aloft
The best plan is to carry a tin can on the end of a stick
This draws their attack while I stoop over the well
The tin rattles with the percussion of their beaks.

A Married Man

A married man, with my heart at peace
A quiet wife and two happy children
I could devote myself to poetry then
And tirelessly tread the bewildering
Mazes of thought – but suddenly I lost
My wife and my children, my heart and my head
And though I have a quiet wife again
And a happy boy by her – the other twain
And their mother haunt me like a ghost
Of which I can never be rid

And if I could I'd be worse than dead
So must I abide and when I would fain
Give my whole mind to my whispering muse
These other voices are always there to confuse
And worry my mind and if I set out
Once more on difficult paths of thought I know
Before my next step or my next suddenly
That awful abyss will open – so you see
For the most part
Though I have regained a little heart
I just sit silent and dare not go.

Against Untempered Light

Ah, temperate light, do not sharpen your rays
Lest each of these dear familiar things
To a caricature of itself
From its normal guise springs.

Too much light is not good, since, increased,
What enables us to see all we see,
Would insubstantialise it instead
And our world cease to be.

A Shetland Cottage

How can I be feebler than my shabby
Little cottage here on the bare hillside
Above the complicated tideways of Yell Sound?
How can I stand less sturdily, less securely
In the blizzard that encompasses all life today,
Everything reduced to the level of a smash-and-grab raid,
Everyone trying to snatch what he can before the crash comes,
Of course, the looting is accompanied by a sentimental chorus
About brotherhood and peace between the nations,
But that deceives no one – not even
The most hysterical advocates of these ideals.
So we all chatter about security and stability,
Yet, look where you will, there is only chaos.

Money. It is the Money Age. Money has become supreme.
There's only one problem recognised today – the economic problem.
No one cares a damn about any of the others.
Consequently, everything that cannot be defended
On rational grounds is going to be swept away.

That is going to make the world hell – for none of the realities
Are capable of a rational justification.
Every other week the papers are full of details
Concerning the most appalling catastrophes
– Earthquakes, massacres, and God knows what.
But no one ever mentions them. They're forgotten instantly.
The only things that are taken seriously are sweepstakes.
But *they* relate to money. Money is the only reality left.
There's no need even to pay lip-service to anything else.

Like a Particle of Bone

Like a particle of bone, a trivial thing in itself,
That falling upon the brain can transform
The best of men into a criminal lunatic
So the nonentity Chamberlain on the British ethos today
Casting off the last shreds of political morality
And elevating an obscene blackmailer
To the dominance of Europe
– In the name of a peace which this monstrous surrender
To violence makes ultimately impossible.
Never were accessories to a crime more cold-blooded;
The callous and irresponsible betrayal
Of the Czech republic has brought not peace
But a new and sharper sword.

Wart-Hogs

Wart-hogs I have called our bourgeoisie;
Comical brutes with short steps and a stuffy, parvenu,
Small-town sufficiency, which at the least alarm
Breaks down completely – O frabjous view! –
And away they scurry, tails held stiffly
Perpendicular, and their short legs row by row
Scrabbling the small stones in a frantic effort
To go faster than nature allows them to go.

You know the King Crab; a green shield which glides,
Half mooches over sand, but if in turning shows
Its legs, there's a horrible confusion of brown stalks.
Just so all modern civilisation goes,
The most polished culture a waste land in below,
But most men have the counter knack it seems
And in their presence every bestial sight
Tucks away its horrors in below and with strange beauty gleams.

All the Welsh Writers in Great Britain Today

To Keidrych Rhys

Thanks to you, all the Welsh writers in Britain today
Have become like the salmon in the River Wye
When that quiet stream suddenly begins to rage
And moorhen nests, and rubbish, and tree-trunks whirl by.

Heedless of any lure, the salmon are at once
Possessed with a sort of mania to rush upstream
Towards the Radnor cloudburst that has caused
This fortuitous flooding. So today all these writers seem.

The War Memorial

We knew them – queer that side by side in the ranks
The immortal heroes alone should all have been slain
And only the worthless, the unemployables, the scum
Like us spared to come home again.

Spared to come home and appreciate to the full
The services our fallen comrades gave.
A country fit for heroes to live in. Certainly
It takes a lot less courage to lie in the grave.

They make a fine fuss about them now they are dead;
If they'd survived it would be a different story.
They would be treated just as we are, like dirt,
With no bunkum at all about honour and glory.

'An ex-soldier?' the employers would have said,
'What the Hell's that to do with us at this time of day?
It's a score of years now since the Armistice,
And time to stop harping on that old lay!'

And by Heaven! If God should be taken in
By the War Memorial piffle some year and relent and send
All the fallen back alive, the hellish hypocrisy
– And (on the boys' bayonets) its makers – would suddenly end.

We'd get the truth about the War then all right.
No politician or brasshat dare show his face
With these repatriated angels about, I bet
– But here the dead can't get a word in edgeways!

While Goering Slept

While Goering slept, too soundly
To feel the itch of them,
Two caterpillars crawled on his face
And started betting which of them
From one end of his mouth could go
Most quickly to the opposite one.
Thrice they went, and the same worm won
Though the other failed to see it run.
Then 'Tell me how you do it, pray?'
'It's easy,' the winner replied, 'By heck!
You go the whole length of the lips. I take
The short cut round the back of the neck.'

On the Imminent Destruction of London, June 1940

Now when London is threatened
With devastation from the air
I realise, horror atrophying in me,
That I hardly care.

The withering in me of the nerve of horror
Is only I see, as it were,
A foreglimpse of the elimination
Of Earth's greatest horror down there.

For if any further place as is inevitable
Must in this way be burst asunder, burned, and lost
It may as well be London as any
– Nay, London far better than most.

Other places may be blasted to bits
And it simply does not matter.
But London, London, what countless shackles
Must with its shattering shatter!

For London is the centre of all reaction
To progress and prosperity in human existence
– Set against all that is good in the spirit of man,
As Earth's greatest stumbling block and rock of offence.

Death and destruction has gone out from London
All over the world. It has sat
Like a gorged spider in the ghastly centre of the web
In which all human hopes like flies are caught.

London has flourished like a foul disease
In the wasting body of the British Isles
And drained all the world's wealth to its pirate's cave
By its callous and cowardly wiles.

The Fall of France

25th June, 1940

The clouds are dark an heavy, but it winna rain, you say.
For they're nae mair than burden notes meant
To show up the better the hie enchantment
O' this soarin' and passionate simmer day.

And, I cry, it's true in juist the same way
O' the terrible treachery and hellish poo'er
That for the moment whummle the pride o' France in the stour
– Burden notes to cast up aye the glory o' Freedom's sway!

I look oot owre the haill earth, seeing
Hoo in reality, gin deeply eneuch ane ponders it,
All, all is beautiful but what we oorsels think and dae wha forget
Oor human dignity and the higher aims o' being.

I look oot owre all creation. My mortal een scan
The unfauldin' space which opens to right an' left an fills me
Wi' that mournfu' exultation peculiar to Man
Wha looks at freedom through the windas o' a body no' free.

The German Bombers

The Second World War, proceeding as I write, has already brought home to big sections of the Scottish population the blackguardly, and, indeed, murderously unscrupulous, attitude towards Scotland of the English government. The following verses comment on one extraordinary example of this and express, I believe, the real state of affairs between England and Scotland today:

The German bombers came up the Forth
And unchallenged all day o'er Edinburgh flew
While not in Edinburgh but only in London
The air-raid warning siren blew.

Scotland might have been shattered to smithereens
For all the English cared, or the Scots themselves dared;
We owe our thanks to German inadvertence,
Not English protection, that Edinburgh was spared.

The English don't give a curse so long as England's all right,
And from Scotland to that end withdraw all Scotland's might
On lying pretexts, while the Scots themselves, poor fools,
Are content in Scotland's betrayal to be England's tools.

The leprous swine in London town
And their Anglo-Scots accomplices
Are, as they have always been,
Scotland's only enemies.

from *Five Minutes' Silence*

'Who has seen the line of bayonets ready to jump the parapet and has not realised how much of the God there is in every man' (General H. Page-Croft, *Twenty-two Months Under Fire*)

It's a long worm that has no turning
But individually these worms are tiny,
Too small to turn,
Though nose of the next to the tail
Of the one before
They stretch out over the whole world
In endless lines
Like processional caterpillars,
Avalanches of maggots, millions of them,
Moving as one.

So I see the armies of the world once more
As I saw them a quarter of a century ago
But despite the many millions killed then
Far more numerous than ever before
Swinging along over scores of countries
Rank after rank
Beneath the drab ill-fitting uniforms,
And it seems to me that I see
Beneath the tough skins
Of the twisted under-nourished little bodies,
Bleached by years of mines and factories,

Into the hearts and beyond even that
Into the womb of time and what it was that made
These countless hordes of gnomes.

I see them born out of the smoke and filth
Of factories, out of the damp and blackness
Of mines, out of starvation and misery
The greed of mankind and the black
Sanctimonious hypocrisy of the nineteenth century.

None of them ever had a chance at life
Nor their fathers and mothers
For generation after generation
Before them, until at last
They have emerged from the womb of time,
Vast armies of men,
Small and wretched and deformed.
Their numbers seem as I look
To multiply vaguely into thousands and millions
Coming not only out of our Black Belts
But out of France and Germany and America and Italy,
From all of the Western world,
Marching and marching, a cloud of men
Till the whole earth and the sky itself
Seems filled with marching men.

And I remember how I too
A quarter of a century ago
Became one man in a similar horde
Not because I was valiant and brave

And full of faith in my action
But carelessly, helplessly until I hoped to be killed
In order that I would no longer
Have to suffer the intolerable sense
Of shame for being a man,
One billionth part of what was called
'The Civilised West'.

Culloden

Yet how can I understand all and forgive all?
      Clouds over Culloden Moor today
Still shape themselves like memories of the bestial face
      That drove all Scotland's light away.

Women and children held in a gross jowl's folds;
      Surely whoever saw these pig's eyes saw
Wanton brutality boast Royalty
      And Scotland mangled in an obscene maw.

Nay, saw the prototype of all the horde
      Of witless generals who since then
Have viciously sacrificed to unknown ends
      The lives of millions of men.

Surely It Were Better

Surely it were better to perish at their hands
Than beat them by outdoing their atrocities
Destroying helpless civilians, women, and children,
While mouthing still all our old hypocrisies.

And sacrificing our young men and even our girls
To put an end, we claim, in Berlin and in Rome
To such systematic violations of all human decency
Our rulers increasingly emulate at home.

Is a Mussolini or a Hitler
Worse than a Bevin or a Morrison
– At least the former proclaim their foul purposes
The latter practise what their words disown.

Bevin or a Morrison: Ernest Bevin (Minister of labour and National Service) and Herbert Morrison (Home Secretary), both leading officers of state in the British government during the Second World War.

A Pair of Fulmar Petrels

I remember seeing a pair of fulmar petrels
Approaching the coast on a stormy day last January
They overcame the gale with scarcely a movement of their long rigid
wings,

Slanting in long, graceful lines to the surface of the sea
And then throwing themselves up exultingly
On the arms of the storm. A wave broke on their course and the wind
Lifted the spray high in a rainbow cloud
Fast as the spray rose heavenward the fulmars
Rose faster. Almost vertically into the sky they rushed,
Their wings all the time motionless, as if
The force of gravity did not exist. Then when the fury
Of the wave had spent itself, they glided gracefully down.
Later I visited their squalid nest on the white-spattered rocks
And I think of these fulmars and the rainbow spray
Whenever I think now of kings and so-called great generals
And how their glory vanishes – how ungainly
At close quarters they are – and how after being borne aloft
So gloriously on the winds of history they are seen
As the dullest of bores and pass into due oblivion.

from *The Monarch of the Glen*

Years ago I felt inclined to sing:
Come on, Christine, Walter, Michael,
Let your spirit be like the deer.
Take your Scotland. England lacks
Any such glorious form as here
An influence to the landscape yields
Almost like trees and fields.

Placeless as the rainbow is
The whole of the countryside is theirs.
Stock keep the plains, blue hares the heights,
This loch or that the great divers.
But the red deer feed here, rest there,
And wander everywhere.

Come on Christine, Walter, Michael,
Be like the deer when it's suddenly stormfast,
With missiles of rain like bullets here,
Patient as a cattle-beast till the onslaught's past
Then shaking itself, lost in a fountain of drops,
Free of water as a seal on a rock when it stops.

Catholic as our country is,
Ranging seashore, valley, and hill,
Where will you find a finer beast
In freer enjoyment still – even still –
Of its native liberty than in Scotland here?
Come on, my children, be like the deer.

But now I know the red deer is a tragic beast.
His life is cast in a lean land
And he is the child of storm and torrent
And old stags die in strange and tragic ways.

Christine, **Walter**, **Michael**: the names of the author's children.

The Doctor and the Minister

What, said the doctor,
Little children at work
In factories and coalmines
From daybreak to mirk
I cannot see, he said,
With his notable charm
Seven days a week of this
Can do them any harm
– Of course it crooks their backbones
And spoils their eyes
And whitens their blood
But it's all right otherwise:
And the minister agreed
Keeps them from mischief he said.

Here, Dust Must Prevail

Here, dust must prevail. It devours housewives
Inevitably as graveyard soil. Sometimes they see,
In a flash of awful perception,
How they have spent their strength and beauty
In the struggle against it;
But they scrub on soap-drunk, embittered and preoccupied,
Sore-eyed, raw-knuckled, enraged and winnowed of hope
And still the smuts drift and the soot
Seeps in and coats everything.
The Comprachicos sealed babies in jars.
The baby grew; the jar stayed rigid.
The child was curiously misshapen; its market value
Increased in proportion to its freakishness.
So Glasgow, swelling to maturity,
Within its narrow boundaries,
Has squeezed itself into queer shapes
– A sign of its enhanced value as real-estate.
And now the baby has outgrown the jar,
Flesh and blood is squashed into odd holes and corners.
Bits of bad land soaked in sour water
And deader than salty Sodom
Oh stench! Oh darkness! Oh black and melancholy
Birthplace under a fog-hazed sun!

Comprachicos: A seventeenth-century band of nomads who bought children and created monsters of them for sale to the aristocracy as novelties. See Victor Hugo, *The Man Who Laughed*, second preliminary chapter.

I Have Succeeded

I have succeeded. See behind me now
The multiplicity of organisations all concerned
With one part or another of that great task
I long ago – almost alone – most imperfectly – discerned
As the all-inclusive object of high Scottish endeavour
The same yesterday and today, and forever.
Fianna Alba and the Saltire Society,
The Scottish Socialist Party and Clann nan Gaidheal,
And a host of others all active today
Where twenty years ago there was not one to see.

I Know That I Was Happy Then

I know that I was happy then
In ways I cannot imagine now
And certainly would not allow
To please me, if they threatened to, again.

River-Side

As a loon I had to tak' owre
The auld man's chair at the table
And kent I'd to keep things gaen'
As weel as I was able.

Sae I never had muckle time
To stand and stare at the water
But I kent I wad if I could
Tho' why was anither matter.

Noo I'm drawn to the river again
And think o' a' I've dune syne
In the forty year that's gane by.

Why do folk stand and stare at the river?
I wonder, because I've never been
Sure why, and 'ud fain ha'e been ane o' them.
                    And sure why.

You Do Not Cease To Be Yourself

You do not cease to be yourself
Though you cease to resemble in any way
The person you were in a photograph taken
Ten years ago, or twenty years say.

You only cease to be yourself
Whenever – and in whatever – you cease to change;
For in that your life ends – it is an instalment of death;
The change of all changes most complete and strange
For when life's changes are over you are indeed
Given over to the endless changes you then need.

Yet fools prate of consistency, pride themselves
On this fixed pose and that, and fear to give
Themselves to the sudden incalculable changes
And would fain remain old photographs of themselves rather than live.

Natural Description

'I wonder why good women like bad men.'
That was a thing she certainly knew
Yet she would never tell any man
Even at her age – which was seventy-two.

Bairns Arena Frightened

Bairns arena frightened when they first
See the haill world transformed by snow
But accept the change and shout delightedly
As out to play in it they go.

This means, I think, that if our hearts are pure
We are prepared for any change at all
Owing no allegiance to the world we know
And always eager to renounce its thrall.

Bairns arena frightened when they first
See the haill world transformed by snow
Tho' they canna foresee it will not last forever
And the status quo ante come buldering through.

buldering: gurgling.

Falkland Chapel

Here's the priest's peep-hole through which he keeks
At a' the fine wimmen as they pass by
To the body o' the kirk. But look at his eye!
For there's God in his mou', – and the deil in his breeks!

The Outlaw

I am the outlawed conscience of Scotland,
The voice that must not be heard,
The bane of all time-servers and trimmers,
Helot-usurpers of the true aristocracy of awareness.

Full of the confidence that is the cure
For cowardice and its twin, conceit.
'De gustibus...' means that properly probed
There can be no two minds; pressed *au fond*, all men agree.

Finding a Name

I always have to find a name
For everything that comes into my life.
Vesuvius is my favourite pipe
Wildfire my pocket knife
But there are countless things in Glasgow
For which I'll never find a name I know
I don't know even what they are
Or what they're for
I've studied them as much as I dare
But I'm constantly encompassed still
By the inscrutable and unnameable
– It isn't fair.

No Flowers at Your Grave

I took no flowers to your grave, alas,
But I was glad to see
A few minute weeds among the grass
Flowering all but unnoticeably
Proportionate to all the consolation and hope
For which my mind and heart has scope.

The Freer Flame

Listen. Countrymen used to take pride and pleasure
In the old art of building a log fire.
The wood had to be seasoned for several years
And the different woods blended on the pyre.

It was usually a fruit such as apple,
Pear or cherry for aroma; then came
Hardwood – oak, ash, or beech – for heat,
And possibly birch for flame.

But poets should apply to their own art
The fact that two trees of the same kind
From a different place show this in their burning –
The one from the higher point burns with the freer flame, you find.

On Abandoning a Controversy

Lightnin' disna strike at cabbages
Sae I, wha played aboot you in my wildfire mood
Restored syne to my proper forked condition
Juist leave you to your fate. That's understood.

Aberfan and Viet-Nam

The disaster that befell
The children of Aberfan
Evoked worldwide sympathy
And much practical help,
Yet the children were overwhelmed
In a moment or two
Without warning – and so without fear.
They suffered no long-drawn-out agony.

The people who were most moved
Were the self-same people
Who for years, without protest, have known
That more innocent children every day
Are being destroyed in Viet-Nam
Death coming to them in its most appalling forms
Transforming happy youngsters instantly
Into lumps of horrible pus
Or fragmentation bombs
Blasting them into mincemeat.
– Yet mankind as a whole does nothing
To end this hellish massacre
Due not to any natural catastrophe
But to the diabolical will
Of power-proud men masking
Their mass-murders with hypocritical claims
About establishing independence and peace.

– The disaster that befell
The children of Aberfan
Is nothing compared with Viet-Nam's
Where there's an Aberfan every day
– Is that nothing to you,
All you people who could stop
This insensate and bestial war
In a moment if with one voice
You condemned its perpetrators?

The black mountain of coal-mine slag
That slid down and buried
The innocent children of Aberfan
Was a trifle compared with the avalanche
Of greed, ignorance, lies and cruelty
Unleashed on the little people of Viet-Nam
By the American war criminals
The sun was not created for men like these
They are monsters of cowardice and weakness
If you let them continue to live
They will only make every situation worse
And remain a constant danger
To everything worthwhile in mankind
– Is it nothing to you?
Is it nothing to you?

Westminster Abbey

'Among those who were shareholders of some branch of the Vickers combine –
in all of them there was a remarkably high percentage of clergymen.'

'Almost five hundred clergymen of the Church of England who hold armament
shares – the Clergy Pension fund, its shareholding ten times as big as that of the
Chairman.' (Robert Neumann's *Zaharoff, the Armament King*)

Who speaks of sacrilege in England's shrine
Where boys are taught sweet Christmas carols to sing
And next forced on to human butchering
And all war's horrors by the same suave swine?
Con men, gangsters, corrupters of youth, condign
Must be the punishment of those who bring
Successive generations to the bloody bull-ring
Blandly in the name of the dud-Divine.

This nightmare shrine through whose foul history
Mass-murderers, usurers, lechers and their molls
Find refuge in th'ecclesiastical fol-de-rols
Of urbane liars mouthing black blasphemy
Put out as patriotism and religion. Return O Christ
And purge this infamous shrine of Hell – disguised.

Ancestors

I sometimes think I see
An ancestor o' mine
Wauken in my bluid again,
His een wi' whisky shine –

'Callant', he says, 'if I hadn't got drunk
That day at Ecclefechan Fair
You'd ha'e been an unco different loon
– And micht never ha'e been there.'

Whisky Soft as a Candle's Flame

Do you remember the orchard at Avrânches,
And the wine we drank in the sunshine?
– It was surely sunshine itself we drank
That day, and not just wine.

But now I am growing old and am glad to know
Here in Scotland we've still many a quiet town
Where the whisky is as soft as a candle's flame
And only slightly warmer going down.

The Last of the Lights

I belonged to a little town
And liked to walk at nights
Out into the dark country roads
Beyond the last of the lights
And what I liked as a boy
Tho' I grow old is still my joy

And now as over the years I look back
It seems each of my companions then
– A girl, the moon, a few stars or the lack
Of any of these were one and the same. – Now again
Content beyond the last light I go, and have
No companion – even myself – in the grave.

Bramble Spray in the Autumn Woods

Do I wish my poetry today to be
Like a star, a mountain, a mighty tree?
No! I am content to have it show
As a few bramble leaves in thinned woodlands do
For the humble bramble seems then to devise
                 Surprise on surprise
In glowing lines of the vines
Canary, scarlet, crimson, claret – a spontaneous access
Of beauty when all else is wan and lifeless.

We Need More Men Like Him

As ready as Lady Godiva
To put all they have on a horse.

Acknowledgements

The following information acknowledges the titles where given by MacDiarmid, the titles which have been supplied by the editors (noting the poems which were untitled in manuscript in square brackets), and the provenance of the texts. All but two are from the National Library of Scotland, Edinburgh. MS numbers for NLS holdings are also noted.

'The Secret Voice' in *The Glasgow Herald*, 3 April 1926; 'Mary Reflects' NLS MS27031 f.241 [in pencil]; 'The Lilypond' [in TS], this version was included in the MS of 'Impavidi Progrediamur' NLS MS27025 f.98; in the MS of 'Mature Art' NLS Acc.12074/1 'The Lilypond' was seen as part of 'Facing the Chair' ff.148–9; 'Mother' in 'Mature Art', NLS Acc. 12074/1 145–6 [in TS]; 'My Follies Are My Studies' [untitled] NLS MS27101 f.4v, ?1939 [in pencil]; 'To Christine' NLS MS27031 f.134r [in pencil] 1930; 'If Christ Rose Today' [untitled] NLS MS27031 f.152r. [in pencil]; 'It's a Fine Thing' [untitled] NLS MS27033 f.10 [in ink]; 'Everything in Edinburgh' [untitled] NLS MS27140 f.18r [in pencil] n.d.; 'Bourgeois Poetry' NLS Acc. 12074/9 [in TS]; 'A Man's a Man' NLS MS27030 f.19v [in pencil]; 'Holiday Plan' NLS MS27031 f.140 [in pencil]; 'On an Opponent of Scots Literature' NLS MS27029 f.12r [in ink]; 'My Ambition' [untitled] NLS MS27032 f.93 [in coloured pencil] on back of envelope postmarked 25 Oct 1938; 'The Whole Keyboard' [untitled] NLS MS27031 144r [in pencil]; 'Candlesmas' NLS MS27030 f.1 [in ink]; '*from* The Dark Whirling Dun' NLS MS27031 ff.104–13 [in biro]; 'The Mouse that Bit the Cat' dated 27 January 1932: University of Delaware Library MS224 Box 1, Folder 6 [in TS]; 'Ex Nihil' NLS MS27030 f.6 [in ink]; 'Working At Last' NLS MS27031 f.32 [in TS]; 'The Logic of Contradiction' [untitled] NLS Acc.12074/1 156–7 [in TS]; 'I Thank God Most' [untitled] NLS MS27029 f.11 [in ink]; 'Of the Cheka's Horrors' [untitled] NLS MS27032 f.162 [in pencil]; 'Even Death Has a Home-Life' NLS MS27032 f.172r [in pencil]; 'Bedrock' NLS MS27030 f.7 [in ink]; 'Vementry' NLS MS27030 ff.9–11 [in ink]; 'When I Go To the Well' [untitled] NLS MS27033 f.45 [in pencil]; 'A Married Man' [untitled] NLS MS27031 ff.135r–136v [in pencil] (this poem was written on the same folded notepaper as early versions of 'To Professor Norman

Kemp Smith' which was enclosed in a letter from Hugh MacDiarmid to W.R. Aitken, 5 August 1937; 'Against Untempered Light' NLS MS27031 f.36r [in ink]; 'A Shetland Cottage' NLS MS27032 f.6r and v [in pencil]; 'Like a Particle of Bone' [untitled] NLS MS27152 f.47a. (the lines were written in coloured pencil on blank spaces of an illustrated letter card from Dughal MacColl, 15 September 1938, at the time of the Empire Exhibition); 'Wart-Hogs' NLS MS27021 f.43 [in TS]; 'All the Welsh Writers in Great Britain Today' NLS MS27031 f.142r [in pencil]; 'The War Memorial' NLS MS27031 f.92 [in pencil]; 'While Goering Slept' NLS MS27030 f.30r [in pencil], Draft NLS MS27089 f.6r; 'On the Imminent Destruction of London, June 1940' NLS MS27031 f.5r and v [in pencil]; 'The Fall of France' NLS MS27031 f.3r and v [in pencil]; 'The German Bombers' [untitled] NLS MS27065 f.44 [in TS]; *from* Five Minutes' Silence' NLS MS27105 ff.18r–19 [in pencil]; 'Culloden' [untitled] NLS MS27031 f.150r [in pencil]; 'Surely It Were Better' [untitled] NLS MS27183 ff.16v–17r [in pencil] (a notebook kept while he was working at Mechan's in 1943); 'A Pair of Fulmar Petrels' [untitled] NLS MS27118 f.9v and inside back cover of a notebook dated '?1942' in NLS Catalogue; *from* The Monarch of the Glen' in 'Mature Art' NLS Acc. 12074/1 150 [in TS]; 'The Doctor and the Minister' [untitled] NLS MS27031 f.137r [in pencil]; 'Here, Dust Must Prevail' [untitled] NLS MS27032 f.191v [in pencil]; 'I Have Succeeded' [untitled] MS27117 f.12r [in pencil] c. 1941–2; 'I Know That I Was Happy Then' [untitled] NLS MS27032 f.140r [in pencil]; 'River-Side' NLS MS27031 f.43 [in biro]; 'You Do Not Cease To Be Yourself' [untitled] NLS MS27065 f.117v [in pencil]; 'Natural Description' NLS MS27133 f.1v [in pencil] ?1949; 'Bairns Arena Frightened' [untitled] NLS MS27032 f.176r [in pencil]; 'Falkland Chapel' NLS MS27031 f.144v [in pencil]; 'The Outlaw' in 'Mature Art' NLS Acc.12074/1 240–1 [in TS]; 'Finding a Name' [untitled] NLS MS27136 f.1r [in pencil] c. 1955; 'No Flowers at Your Grave' [untitled] NLS MS27138 f.68r [in pencil] 1958; 'The Freer Flame' [untitled] NLS MS27031 f.95 [in pencil]; 'On Abandoning a Controversy' NLS MS27031 f.155r [in pencil]; 'Aberfan and Viet-Nam' [untitled] NLS MS27031 f.220r and v [in biro]; 'Westminster Abbey' in *The National Weekly*, 20 January 1951; 'Ancestors' [untitled] NLS MS27031 f.141r [in pencil]; 'Whisky Soft as a Candle's Flame' [untitled] NLS MS27031 f.168r [in ink]; 'The Last of the Lights' [untitled] NLS MS27032 f.23r [in pencil] written on the back of the start of a letter from Michael Grieve to W.R. Aitken ('Uncle Bill') in ink c. 1940; 'Bramble Spray in the Autumn Woods' NLS MS27101 f.8v [in pencil] ?1939; 'We Need More Men Like Him' [untitled] NLS MS27096 f.28v [in pencil]. These lines are also given as a single line in NLS MS27029 f.27 and f.43, two 'Glasgow' MSS, where the context is: 'As the shopkeepers and the street-corner keelies / All as ready as Lady Godiva to put all they have on a horse'.

The editors gratefully acknowledge the professionalism and generosity of the staff of the National Library of Scotland, Edinburgh. Poems from the NLS archives are published by kind permission of the Trustees of the National Library of Scotland. 'The Mouse that Bit the Cat' is published by permission of the University of Delaware Library.

John Manson was the recipient of a grant from the Scottish Arts Council Professional Development Fund, for which we are most grateful.

The editors would like to thank Ms Helen Lloyd for her help in scanning and formatting the poems from typescript to disk. Thanks are also due to William Neill for providing the glossary for 'My Ambition'. We are grateful to Lida Moser for the frontispiece portrait photograph. Special thanks are due to Ken Currie for allowing us to reproduce as our cover a detail from a panel of his mural in the People's Palace, Glasgow, 'The Great Reform Agitation… Union is Strength'.

Publication of this book was assisted by the Department of Scottish Literature at the University of Glasgow.